D0833511

Family Business Ownership:
How To Be An
Effective
Shareholder

Craig E. Aronoff, Ph.D. and
John L. Ward, Ph.D.

Family Business Leadership Series, No. 15

Family Enterprise Publishers
P.O. Box 4356
Marietta, GA 30061-4356
800-551-0633
www.efamilybusiness.com

ISSN: 1071-5010
ISBN: 1-891652-05-2
© 2002
Third Printing

Family Business Leadership Series

We believe that family businesses are special, not only to the families that own and manage them but to our society and to the private enterprise system. Having worked and interacted with hundreds of family enterprises in the past twenty years, we offer the insights of that experience and the collected wisdom of the world's best and most successful family firms.

This volume is a part of a series offering practical guidance for family businesses seeking to manage the special challenges and opportunities confronting them.

To order additional copies, contact:
Family Enterprise Publishers
1220-B Kennestone Circle
Marietta, Georgia 30066
Tel: 1-800-551-0633
Web Site: www.efamilybusiness.com

Quantity discounts are available.

Other volumes in the series include:

Contents

Exhibits

Introduction:
On Being an Owner

If you are a shareholder in your family's business, this booklet is for you—no matter how many or how few shares you own, whether or not you work in the business and regardless of how you came by your shares.

Being an owner of a family business should be a satisfying, fulfilling, and profitable experience. For some, however, ownership is represented by a stock certificate, a "piece of paper" that has little meaning. For others, ownership leads to grief, conflict, and frustration. Owners who are managers employed in the business may feel unappreciated and may be distrustful of or even disdainful toward owners outside the business. At the same time, owners outside the business may feel treated inequitably, concerned that they aren't getting enough attention, appreciation, or dividends or that information is being withheld from them. Younger shareholders may be confused about their roles and responsibilities and feel inadequate to the task of ownership. Still others may be simply overwhelmed by anything "financial" and try to avoid having to deal with ownership issues altogether.

For too many shareholders, being an owner just isn't any fun. But it could be. In fact, it could be one of the most rewarding experiences of your life—and we don't mean just financially.

For some individuals, ownership is all about money—the dividends they receive, the frustration they feel at having their funds tied up in the business, or, if they're managers, the stress of trying to improve the bottom line so that cantankerous shareholders are mollified and the business can grow.

But, in our view, ownership can mean more than monetary rewards. It can return to you and your family much more—spiritually, psychologically, intellectually, and emotionally—than mere cash.

While not underestimating the importance of financial return, we may challenge your ideas about ownership. We hope to offer some insights that can make your experience as an owner take on a whole new meaning and transform your thinking, so that being an owner of a family business becomes one of the most worthwhile aspects of your life.

Ownership, at its best, means stewardship—protecting and nurturing the family business and preserving it for the benefit of the next generation of family members and for employees, customers, and the community. As such, ownership can be a vehicle for adding purpose to one's life; for being a better parent, spouse, brother or sister, son or daughter,

1

uncle or aunt or cousin; for enhanced performance as a manager or a strategic decision maker inside or outside the business; and for providing an opportunity for service.

This booklet will help you develop yourself as an effective family business owner. It will show you why family business ownership can be good for the business and good for the family. It will help you understand your role as an owner. You will gain the knowledge needed to become more valuable as an owner. You will also discover how to manage some of the most difficult issues that face family business owners, as well as how to prepare the next generation for their responsibilities as future owners. The glossary beginning on page 60 will help you understand many of the terms used on these pages, and a section on Suggested Readings and Resources will lead you to materials that will expand on what you learn here.

We think this book can be a vital tool for any family business owner. However, our guess is that it will prove most useful and valuable to those shareholders who see ownership in a family business as a privilege, who regard the family business as a noble institution, and who have a well-developed interest in and concern for the welfare of others.

One of our most important aims, however, is to help bring about greater harmony between two sets of owners: those who are employed as managers in the family business and those who are not. These two groups often have disparate interests and perspectives. When each speaks the same language as knowledgeable owners, and when all seek understanding of and empathy for their fellow owners, the family and the business are both better served.

This book is NOT a technical or legal treatise on how to set up buy-sell agreements, establish a valuation method for the business, or the like. We urge you to see your attorney and your financial advisor for such matters. We will give you the language and the concepts to make those discussions more efficient and productive. Furthermore, if you follow the principles outlined here, this book WILL provide a philosophical foundation that will support the decisions you make about technical and legal issues. It will enable you more consciously to integrate your values into the technical decisions that you make and the agreements that you develop.

Chances are you didn't choose to become an owner. Owners who founded their businesses could be said to have volunteered for ownership. So could individuals who bought shares from other family members. **By the time you get to the second or third generation of a family-held business, however, owners generally are individuals who inherited their slice of the family business pie. Often heirs feel**

unworthy or undeserving of ownership because they have not earned it. If you are such an heir, this booklet will address some of those emotional issues and help you resolve them.

In our minds, however, heirs become deserving of ownership and turn it into a voluntary act by stepping up to their responsibilities. They study, they learn, they participate, they look out not just after their own interests but the interests of the business and the family. In short, they transform themselves into **effective** owners. This book will show you how. Ultimately, it is designed to help all shareholders understand how they can be as constructive and as contributing and as responsible and as fulfilled as they can be in their role as owners. It is aimed at helping shareholders find a higher purpose as owners. It is about making ownership work.

Heirs become deserving of ownership and turn it into a voluntary act by stepping up to their responsibilities

II. What Is a Family Business Owner?

Legally speaking, if you possess even one share of a family business, you are an owner. There are different categories of ownership, however, and different situations and conditions that affect ownership. We will get into these. We will also talk about what owners deserve—as owners—and about some of the limitations of ownership.

"Good" family business owners, no matter what category of ownership they fall into or how few or how many shares they own, do the long, hard (and rewarding) work of ownership. They are **involved**, in the best sense of the word. They help nurture and guide the relationship between the family and the business, and may make some sacrifices or some tough decisions in the best interests of both. They are concerned, in a way that goes beyond narrow self-interest, about the future of the family business and the family.

Owners versus Investors

While owners are investors in the sense that they have at-risk assets tied up in a business, an investor and an effective family business owner are not the same. Investors are people who are simply risking their money in hopes of a good financial return. They are not really personally or emotionally involved with the company in which they are investing. Typically, they do not personally identify with the business in which they have invested.

While owners are investors in the sense that they have at-risk assets tied up in a business, an investor and an effective family business owner are not the same.

Being an effective business owner is a more intimate matter. Suppose you buy some shares in a natural gas company. Soon after, a number of employees are killed in an explosion involving one of the company's pipelines. Even though you have an investment in that company, does knowing about the explosion and its consequences bother you any more than learning about some other disaster? Probably not, because you don't really have any personal connection to it.

On the other hand, if you own stock in your family business and there is a similar disaster, you will most likely feel it very deeply. The company and your family may share the same name. If you are an involved, effective owner—that is, a "good" owner—you may actually know some of the victims of the disaster. Even if you don't, you will feel a sense of responsibility to and caring about the employees and their families. It becomes very personal.

The danger is that as family businesses move from generation to generation, ownership becomes depersonalized if a family is not vigilant or fails to take preventive action. By the third or fourth generation, there can be many owners. Most will have inherited or married in, and some may feel that "we're only here for the financial return." Others may object, saying, "No, we have a legacy here. We have a personal connection. We have responsibilities."

As authors Robert M. Blonchek and Martin F. O'Neill say in their book, *Act Like an Owner* (John Wiley & Sons, Inc., 1999):

> "You don't create *owners* by giving people stock—you create *investors*. Think about the personal investments you may have in publicly traded companies. Do you feel any sort of accountability to help those companies perform? Sure, you *want* the companies to perform—you probably *demand* that they perform. But you probably don't feel accountable for the performance of the businesses. . . .Investors hold *management* accountable for business performance, not themselves."

The continued success of a family business requires active teamwork involving owners, managers, and the board of directors. A business family that slides into a situation where owners think mainly like investors can expect trouble.

If you are an owner who feels and acts exclusively like an investor, it's time to consider your choices. You can take a greater interest in the business and turn yourself into an effective owner. Or (and hopefully the family will bless this decision and make it possible), you can divest yourself of your stock and invest the proceeds elsewhere. If your motivation is purely financial while the bulk of the shareholders' motivations include other goals besides financial ones, you're just not on the same page. There's nothing wrong with having different motivations. But **when some owners' goals are not in alignment with those of most of the other owners, serious conflict and damage can ensue.**

The continued success of a family business requires active teamwork involving owners, managers, and the board of directors.

5

Likewise, a group of owners may sense that some of its members are interested only in financial return and not in the other factors that move a business forward—family culture, strategic planning for the business and the family, contribution to the community and so on. If that is the case, the committed owners should make it possible for the less-interested ones to exit ownership. [The concept of "graceful exits" is further discussed in Chapter VII.)

Types of Owners and Forms of Ownership

Owners sit at the top of the pyramid in a family business. They choose who will sit on the board of directors. The board, in turn, chooses and oversees management:

From a legal standpoint, the types of family business owners can be described as follows:

—**Majority and Minority Owners.** A majority owner is one who controls more than half of a company's voting shares. He or she can outvote other owners and is therefore said to be a controlling owner. Majority owners may use their voting power to control major decisions for the company.

Minority shareholders own less than half the shares. In companies where there is no clear majority—where stock is split equally among three siblings or five cousins, for example—some owners can band together to outvote other owners, unless stock ownership is divided into voting shares and non-voting shares.

—**Voting and Non-voting Owners.** Many a founder has worked with his or her lawyer to pass on shares of the business to children without passing on control. Such founders reason that as long as they are alive, they want to be in charge. So two classes of stock are set up—voting and non-voting, sometimes called Class A and Class B. The parent retains the voting stock and passes the non-voting stock on to the kids. It's not unusual for the next generation to own most of the stock while a parent retains control of the company through his or her voting shares. (Similar techniques are also used by family businesses that are publicly traded. For example, the family may retain the voting shares with only non-voting shares available to investors from outside the family. The family may choose to retain a block of stock so large that it effectively serves as a barrier to outsiders gaining control.)

—**General Partners and Limited Partners.** When family businesses are structured as partnerships, a general partner has voting power; limited partners do not. General partners (and there may be more than one in a business) have unlimited personal liability, while limited partners can lose only what they have invested in the business. We will treat partners as shareholders in this book.

People who are not typical owners but who must be considered in this discussion are **trustees** and **beneficiaries.** Some shares in a family business may be held in trust for the benefit of an individual or individuals known as beneficiaries. Control of the trust is in the hands of a person or institution designated as the trustee.

Even though the beneficiaries are not owners and do not enjoy voting power, in many cases we consider the next generation members whose shares are held in trust to be "like owners." Under such circumstances, we recommend that they be treated like owners and given all the respect and consideration due an owner. Likewise, **we urge trust beneficiaries to act like owners, taking an interest in and becoming knowledgeable about the business, and participating in family meetings and family councils.** The enhanced relations between the legal owners and the beneficiaries that will result will benefit both the business and the family. In addition, the beneficiaries will gain a greater sense of connection to the business that their granddaddy or great granddaddy started. They will not only benefit financially from their asset; they will receive some psychic income and feel more worthy of their inheritance.

Similarly, many family businesses give consideration to future or intended owners. These people typically are younger-generation family members who are preparing for their inheritance. While neither officially owning shares nor having the rights and responsibilities of ownership, they may be encouraged to develop the knowledge and attitudes of "good" owners.

Types of Owners—Another Perspective

The types of owners described above represent legal and technical distinctions. There are other ways of categorizing owners as well. A given shareholder can fit in more than one of the categories:

—**Operating Owners.** The operating owner is an owner-manager or employed owner with direct responsibility for the business. He or she is a hands-on owner who is in the business every day, helping to run it and make decisions.

—**Governing Owners.** These individuals work not as operators but as overseers—watching, learning, and keeping tight, supportive relationships with management. Governing owners may also be employed in the business, but when they are, they are not in an operating position. Instead, they would be an equivalent to the board chair, a director or a corporate ombudsman.

Governing owners typically are very knowledgeable about the strategic issues confronting the business and often help to shape corporate strategy. They are also active in shaping the culture of the organization by virtue of their presence, their behavior, or their interests.

—**Active Owners.** These owners are not employed in the business and may not even be on the business site very often. However, they are **attentive to the issues facing a family business**. They develop relationships with management, they make it a point to understand the company strategy, and they take the time to promote the culture of the business. In other words, they take a genuine interest in the company, offer support to management, and involve themselves as appropriate.

—**Proud Owners.** These owners may not be engaged in the business, its board, or its management. They don't really understand its strategy, they're not knowledgeable about its governance, and they don't really feel comfortable around the business. Nevertheless, they are proud to be owners, they read the information that is sent to them, and they attend what family business-related events they can. They take joy in what they own.

—**Passive Owners.** In our view, passive owners are often just along for the ride. They are happy to receive the benefits of ownership but don't acknowledge their responsibilities. They typically pay little attention, and neither educate themselves about the business nor participate in it, except perhaps to express largely uninformed opinions. They merely collect dividends, abdicating responsibility for the business to others.

—**Investor Owners.** Investors are very much like passive owners except that, if they are satisfied or dissatisfied with their returns, they may make a deliberate decision to keep or to sell their ownership. They do not take a personal interest in the company nor become involved in strategy.

What kind of an owner are you? If you are reading this booklet, you are probably an owner-operator, a governing owner, an involved owner, or maybe even a proud owner.

What Family Business Owners Deserve

Every owner has certain legal rights—for example, if they have voting stock, the right to vote their shares. In a family business, however, where intimacy and emotion co-exist with bottom lines and strategic planning, it's much more important to consider what owners—ALL owners— deserve and should expect from their position as shareholders. Ideally, family business owners deserve:

A Financial Return. Ownership means having one's capital at risk. Some family businesses fail to reward ownership with either dividends or the opportunity to sell shares. Some family firms make working for the business the only path to financial reward, a dangerous approach that confuses ownership and employee rewards unless ownership is restricted to those who work in the business. While family businesses often have goals in addition to financial return, a tangible financial reward is an appropriate

> *Some family firms make working for the business the only path to financial reward, a dangerous approach that confuses ownership and employee rewards.*

9

expectation for owners of any business asset.

Leadership. Ownership, the board, and management should make a priority of leadership development and succession planning to assure that the necessary competence, trustworthiness, and vision will be available to nurture company growth and success.

Information. Shareholders deserve adequate information from the management and board of directors. Further, shareholders deserve "transparency" from management—that is, managers need to be open about their plans, pay and performance. Management that is miserly and secretive with information breeds distrust on the part of shareholders who do not work in the business. We discuss this critical issue at length in Chapter VIII.

Psychic Income. In addition to financial reward, family business owners deserve a sense of belonging and a sense of purpose as a result of their ownership. They should be able to feel that they are participating in and contributing to the success of the enterprise. Psychic income is an important and unique bonus of family business ownership. **If you as an owner are not experiencing psychic income or if, worse, you feel a real sense of emotional cost as an owner, then something is wrong and needs to be addressed.** (Unfortunately, we find that in some family businesses, owners are expected to subsist entirely on psychic income. We don't think that's appropriate either.)

Accountability. Shareholders need to be able to hold management and the board of directors (and each other) accountable in a number of dimensions, among them:

1. *A set of values.* Management should be able to demonstrate that it is running the company in accordance with values set forth by the family. (See Family Business Leadership Series #12, "Family Business Values: How To Assure a Legacy of Continuity and Success.")

2. *Performance standards.* The board and top executives need to articulate what ownership can expect in terms of short-term and long-term performance. Goals relating to profitability, return on investment, growth, and other financial criteria should be made clear, with results reported on a timely basis.

3. *Processes that assure accountability.* There should be a board of directors with independent board members on it, as well as rules, policies and procedures that govern the processes.

4. *Non-financial goals.* The desire for financial return is a given. However, family businesses have other goals as well—in such areas as innovation, employee relations, community relations, and

philanthropy. Accountability needs to be established for non-financial goals as well as for financial ones.

A Board of Directors. We think business owners deserve a competent board that includes exemplary independent directors—business leaders from other companies who can complement your team and help you take your business where you want it to go. (In the process, they'll help increase the financial reward to owners.) As we discuss at length in Chapter V, the board has fiduciary responsibility for the business and represents the ownership group as a whole.

Respect. This includes an honest effort to be listened to and responded to, in terms of your goals as an owner. Owners deserve to be taken seriously and to be heard (although they cannot always expect to have their way). Respect also means that **the business should not be used to attempt to control the behavior of adult shareholders** by playing favorites with jobs or perks or manipulating dividends.

A business-owning family needs to find a balance among the freedom of the individual, the welfare of all shareholders, and the integrity of the business.

Protection for the Business. Family business assets represent long-term commitments. Few family businesses can offer to redeem shares at a shareholder's discretion. Shareholders should not be permitted to put the business at risk by giving or selling their stock to inappropriate owners. Shareholder agreements should be developed to deal with such issues. A business-owning family needs to find a balance among the freedom of the individual, the welfare of all shareholders, and the integrity of the business

EXHIBIT 2 ▰▰▰▰▰▰▰▰▰▰▰▰▰

What Owners Deserve

- *Leadership*
- *Psychic and financial returns*
- *A competent board of directors*
- *Protection for the business*

- *Information*
- *Accountability*
- *Respect*

The Limitations of Family Business Ownership

For all its pluses—financial reward, proud connection with an institution, the opportunity to participate in something larger than oneself—family business ownership does have some down sides. The most obvious is the limitation on the liquidity of your shares. You can't call your stockbroker with a sell order like you can with stock in publicly traded companies.

Another potential down side of being a family business owner is that families, in an effort to protect the business and family reputation, often place limits on shareholders' behavior. In effect, they say, "You're expected to behave in certain ways in public, you're expected to behave in certain ways toward the business, and you're expected to behave in certain ways in developing your career." **Members of business-owning families often struggle with conflicts between family desires for conformity and personal desires for individuality and independence.**

To cope with such conflicts, some families draw up a code of conduct; a document outlining expected standards of behavior. We believe this is a good idea, as long as everyone involved gets to participate in the development or revision of such codes and agrees to abide by them.

A little-recognized but important danger is that having a substantial part of their wealth tied up in the ownership of a family business renders some people incapable of becoming independent of family. Others allow themselves to become infantilized by their families. Not only are they financially dependent but they rely on and defer to the family, assuming a "Father knows best" attitude.

Having some degree of liquidity is important because it lets people make decisions about their own spending and their own money, instead of returning again and again to the business or the family for funds.

Individual shareholders and families need to come to terms with these dependency issues. Adult family members should take responsibility for themselves and the family, as a whole must encourage its members to do so, telling them: "Make yourself a good life. Be useful, and make your ownership something that contributes toward achievement rather than something that allows you to coast through life."

The Effect of Dispersed Ownership or Being Publicly Traded

Ownership challenges change as a family grows larger. In some respects, the issues become both easier and harder.

When shareholders are few, individual owners are more conspicuous and feel more empowered. Communication is easier in the sense that a small group—a sibling team, perhaps—can all get in one room, toss the issues around, and work things out. At the same time, each owner carries heavier burdens than do individuals in a larger shareholder group.

Suppose you are one of three equal owners. Your brother and sister work in the business but you have a career elsewhere. Even though you don't work in the company, you have a huge burden because, as an owner, you need to achieve a high level of effectiveness. If you're an uninformed owner, you are much more likely to hold a company back than you would be in a larger family, where you would likely own a much smaller percentage of its stock and where responsibility would be shared among many more people.

The smaller the number of owners, the greater the ability of an individual or a small group of individuals to enhance company progress or create a threat. If a rift occurs and one of four equal shareholders wants out, the other three may find it difficult or impossible to redeem his 25 percent without damage to the company's financial structure.

In a larger shareholder group, dependency on any one individual is reduced since ownership and power is dispersed. If a shareholder wants out, a smaller percentage of the company's capital is required to redeem his or her shares, so it is easier to find the necessary funds.

The more owners there are, the more distance and disconnection from the business many may feel. It becomes necessary to reach out and nurture shareholders, encouraging them to become effective owners and, as this booklet suggests, offering them resources to do so. "Shareholder relations" becomes important, even in a privately owned business.

Ownership issues change again if a family business becomes a publicly traded, family-controlled company. Now you have a market that sets the stock prices, and the family has a safety valve it did not have before: the opportunity to sell shares on the open market.

In a publicly traded company, the fiduciary responsibility of the management and the board extends to others beyond the family. Theoretically and legally, the business no longer responds to just the family. Management and the board are expected to consider the goals

The interests and goals of family shareholders are very different from those of public shareholders. Serving both groups is usually a considerable challenge.

of all owners, and may find that the interests and goals of family shareholders are very different from those of public shareholders. Serving both groups is usually a considerable challenge.

Family members will often find that they are not able to get as much information or get it as early because of the laws regulating publicly traded companies. Their company will get greater scrutiny from the stock exchange and the Securities and Exchange Commission. Family shareholders can no longer assume special privileges just by being family members or in control. In short, **publicly traded companies, lose freedom in terms of how the business is managed but gain freedom through liquidity and access to capital.**

As this chapter suggests, ownership in a family business is a complicated affair. Even if you're a relatively uninvolved owner, there are forces at work that affect you: the quality of the management and the board, harmony or disharmony in the family, aspirations of family members for financial reward, and even the distribution of ownership and the size of the ownership group.

Being a good owner is even more complex. It means looking at all the issues related to family business and playing a role, in concert with management, the board, and other family owners, in their resolution. **A good owner is a person who makes a conscious decision to be an effective participant and contributor to the family business and to the business family.**

You don't have to work in the business to be an effective owner—you can play outside support roles that are of great value to its success. Doing so, however, takes time, energy, and effort—to learn what you need to know, to keep up with the information that you need to have, and to spend time interacting with other family members around the issues that the business faces.

III. The Power of Cohesive Ownership

Families can be good for the businesses they own, and businesses can be good for the families that own them—particularly when owners pull together in the same direction. Like one hand washing the other, a business can provide the cohesive focus that brings a family together, and the family cohesion, in turn, benefits the business and moves it forward.

Many forces work to pull today's families apart—psychological pressures, careers that take younger family members around the world, the desire of individuals for independence, affluence, mobility, and much more. If families want to remain cohesive, they often need something that pulls them back together. Common ownership of and involvement with a business can help to serve that purpose.

Benefits to the Family

A 63-year-old business founder was meeting with three sons and a daughter, each involved in various aspects of their family company. They addressed various opportunities and problems. Sophisticated analyses were offered on investments. Personal issues were discussed. The company's efforts to manage some difficult computer problems were reviewed. "Being here and doing this with my children—it's great," said the founder. "I just hope they get to do this with their kids."

The chance to work with family. The chance to put cherished beliefs into practice. The chance to serve society. The chance to provide a positive example to others. And making money, too. That's what family business is all about.

Owning a business gives family members something to work on as a group, offering them a shared sense of responsibility and pride. And notice that we said "work on," not "work in." As a family grows larger over the generations, more and more of its members will have careers, employment, or interests outside the business but will also own shares in it. These outside owners can work "on" the family business side by

Owning a business gives family members something to work on as a group, offering them a shared sense of responsibility and pride.

15

side with the inside owners, enhancing its chances for continued success.

Business ownership gives family members a mechanism through which they can fulfill their aspirations. A business offers them opportunities not only for employment but also for leadership in both the family and the company. A successful business also brings esteem to the family and provides it with opportunities it would not otherwise have for philanthropy and for service to the family and the community.

Through their businesses, many families come into contact with stimulating leaders in other businesses, in their industry, or in their community. When their business requires travel, they enjoy opportunities for exposure to people and places all over the world.

By their very existence, businesses encourage family owners and managers to consciously articulate values, instill discipline in family members, nurture good judgment about the world at large, and engage in long-term thinking. These actions are a plus in any family but are, we think, more likely to occur in a family that tends a business.

Benefits to the Business

Research shows that family-owned businesses outperform and outlast other forms of businesses. We think that's because a cohesive family brings to its business a depth and richness that other businesses lack. It brings continuity. It brings commitment and loyalty. It brings identity. It brings culture. It brings a deep caring by a team of people who are aligned in values and goals and share a long-term view. It brings resources. It attracts the energy of the next generation of young people who have already spent most of their lives internalizing key values and behaviors perhaps in preparation to lead the business. When you ask business leaders in successor generations how they learned to be business leaders, they inevitably say, "I learned at the dinner table."

Having the support of unified family ownership allows management to pursue unique long-term strategies giving business competitive opportunities and advantages.

A large consumer products company we know is operated consistent with the family's strong religious principles, which are centered on respect for the Sabbath, dietary laws, corporate and personal tithing, and application of the Golden Rule in employee and community relations. When a third generation family member addressed a family meeting, he put it plainly: "Without the unified commitment of our family shareholders, we couldn't run our business as we do. And no one else would run this business consistent with our values and beliefs.''

Having the support of unified family ownership allows management to pursue unique long-term strategies giving business competitive opportunities and advantages. A family business might invest money in building the enterprise when the market is down, or pursue a diversification strategy when others in its industry are getting back to "core" businesses. Family support enabled William Clay Ford Jr., chairman of the Ford Motor Company, to stand up and say auto makers need to be more environmentally sound even though he is in an industry not known for environmental advocacy.

With cohesive family support, management has the strength to weather a long economic cycle while implementing a given strategy—instead of being pushed year after year to meet the demands placed on it by anonymous shareholders. They aren't forced by Wall Street to pursue growth to the company's detriment. (Consider the multitude of major bankruptcies in recent years among publicly traded movie theater chains that were forced to over-expand in the effort to meet shareholders' growth expectations.)

The Kohler Co., based in Kohler, WI., is famous for its bathroom fixtures. But the company, now more than 125 years old, is a conglomerate with businesses that include furniture, cabinetry, hospitality, and real estate. A *Forbes* magazine profile on the company several years ago, stated, "Kohler Co. probably owes its success to having remained a family company. From the beginning the Kohlers. . . reinvested in the business even at times when other pastures may have looked greener. It wasn't just their capital that was at stake. It was their heritage.''

Another result of cohesive family ownership is the lower cost of capital, at least in the short-to-intermediate term. We call this the "family effect'' and it is discussed at greater length in "Financing Transitions: Managing Capital and Liquidity in the Family Business,'' #7 in the Family Business Leadership Series. Briefly, it is the degree to which family shareholders perceive the value of family heritage and control. When family shareholders are united and committed, they are willing to be more patient and temper their expectations of financial return. Conversely, the cost of capital rises when family conflict leads owners to perceive risks and view rewards as primarily financial.

Ownership Matters

We have had an opportunity to observe a number of businesses that have lasted 100 years or more and we have come to the conclusion that **ownership matters**. We believe that those who stay as owners of a

EXHIBIT 3 ██████████████████████████████████

Benefits of Family Business Ownership

For Families:

- *Provides a cohesive focus that brings family together.*
- *Offers family members a shared sense of responsibility.*
- *Serves as a source of family pride.*
- *Gives the family a means of putting values into action.*
- *Helps family members develop leadership skills.*
- *Makes life more interesting.*
- *Builds wealth.*

For Businesses:

- *Enables a company to outperform and outlast other businesses.*
- *Provides support through the deep caring of a team of people aligned in values and goals.*
- *Assures continuity through long-range vision and family's desire to pass the business to future generations.*
- *Enjoys a corporate culture grounded on conscious values.*
- *Receives the trust of the community based on its identification with the family.*

---

business for a century or more provide important, powerful lessons. Such owners act as stewards. They measure stock turnover in generations, focus on the long term, and are distinctly concerned about the institution they will leave behind.

They show care for their assets, building them for their progeny and for the benefit of all. They understand in their marrow what "Built To Last" means and recognize that while financial value is important, it is only one of the values that provide the foundations for the institutions their families own. They understand that legacy is comprised not just of material goods but also of spiritual values.

Legacy is comprised not just of material goods but also of spiritual values.

Robert Mondavi, founder of the Robert Mondavi Winery in Oakville, CA., speaks of the importance of family ownership in his book, *Harvests of Joy: My Passion for Excellence* (Harcourt Brace & Co., 1998): "My family and I had worked for thirty years to learn wine making from the roots up, to develop our sales and distribution network, establish our name and credibility in the marketplace, and earn our stripes by delivering a top-quality product, year in, year out. Show me a conglomerate with that kind of patience and dedication!"

IV. The "Ownership Attitude"

When you act like an owner—that is, a **good** owner—you accept a host of interesting and challenging responsibilities. You adopt what we call an "ownership attitude." If we had to describe what an ownership attitude means in one word, we'd say **stewardship.**

"Stewardship" is a word so rich with meaning that most have difficulty describing its fullness. The definition that, to our minds, comes closest is: "a person morally responsible for the careful use of money, time, talents, or other resources, especially. with respect to the principles or needs of a community or group." Another significant definition speaks of stewardship as "the individual's responsibility to manage his life and property with proper regard to the rights of others."

Some words stand out in these definitions—morally responsible, careful, respect, needs of community or group, rights of others—all are important to our concept of stewardship as it relates to family business ownership.

In some moving passages in her book, *Personal History* (Alfred A. Knopf, Inc., 1997), the late Katharine Graham describes the beginning of her transition from a somewhat passive owner to an effective operating owner of The Washington Post Co. The suicide of her husband, Phil, who had been running the company, had thrust her from being primarily a homemaker into the top leadership role in the business she inherited. She writes that a board member recalled better than she did what she said when she addressed the board on the day before Phil's funeral: "You said that you wanted to make it clear that [the company] was not for sale, no part of it was for sale, this was a family enterprise and there was a new generation coming along."

Graham says that her four children were "what led me, however hesitantly, to the decision I made then: to try to hold on to the company by going to work."

She didn't realize the enormity of the task before her, how tough it would be, or how frightened she would feel. "Nor did I realize how much I was eventually going to enjoy it all."

As the world knows, Graham didn't just maintain the company, she significantly improved its performance. In her corner, she writes, was an important asset: "my passionate devotion to the company and to the *Post.* I cared so much about the paper and about keeping it in the family that, despite my lack of knowledge and feelings of insecurity, I felt I *had* to make it work."

In terms of ownership, several aspects of Graham's story are significant. By her own admission, she was scared, she was ignorant about running a business, she made mistakes, and she often felt foolish and distressed. But she was passionate about the enterprise and about her family. She had a sense of responsibility to the company and its stakeholders—including employees and the readers served by such holdings as The *Washington Post* and *Newsweek*. She spent countless hours educating herself about the business. She grew to love what she was doing, and she recognized the rewards that she received as an owner and leader—fame, wealth, influence, and the opportunity to interact with world leaders.

Most business owners won't be called upon to make the sacrifices Mrs. Graham did as an owner, and most lives won't be so dramatic. But her story should inspire owners and show them that, if they are confused and overwhelmed by the prospects of ownership, they CAN learn about the business and grow into their responsibilities. And they don't have to do it overnight.

Characteristics of Effective Owners

The cartoon on the following page, featuring characters from *Highlights for Children*, a magazine published by the third generation of the Myers family in Columbus, Ohio, quickly illustrates the difference between an effective owner and one who isn't. We have been observing family business owners for many years and find that the best ones share many of the same traits and habits:

They care about the business. They see the family business as a noble institution, one that is valuable to the community and that is an heirloom for the family. The business means something to them personally and they gain a sense of purpose from it.

They try to add value to the institution. Effective owners seek agreement with one another so that all can speak with one voice. They respect others—management, employees, directors, customers, suppliers, and so forth—who contribute to the business's success. They are clear and consistent about their expectations. They behave in a trustful way so that others know they can be depended on. They have a long-term commitment.

Effective owners seek agreement with one another so that all can speak with one voice.

They contribute to family cohesiveness. They participate in the family process, attending family meetings and taking on family committee assignments. They value the family and demonstrate that value through action. They have fun with the family.

21

Goofus and Gallant in the Family Business

Goofus promotes himself for a seat on the board.

Gallant suggests a CEO from a larger firm in a related industry as director.

Goofus campaigns for higher dividends.

Gallant wants assurance that the company's capitalization is healthy.

Goofus lets other employees know that he's one of the owners.

Gallant insists that he should get no special considerations as an employee.

Goofus pays no attention to the company's financial reports to stockholders.

Gallant works hard to understand the numbers in his financial report.

Goofus skips family meetings and ignores his relatives.

Gallant actively participates in family meetings and builds positive relationships with family members.

Reprinted with permission Highlights for Children

They become independent of their families. Earlier, we discussed the danger of family members becoming infantilized by and dependent on the family when their wealth is tied up in ownership of the business. Wise owners seek their independence, just as any adult should. They find other sources of income, such as through a career, so they do not have to depend on hoped-for dividends from their shares. They focus on responsibilities rather than rights and are more likely to ask, "How can I help?" than "What do I get?"

They educate themselves. They seek knowledge. They search out leaders in the business or the family and ask for help in learning the business. They interview older employees about the business. They attend investment seminars or courses on finance for non-financial managers. They read books about business in general and family business in particular.

They set out to be a force for good. Effective owners seek to do the right thing and to look out for the welfare of others—including other shareholders, the business itself as an institution, the employees, and the community. They make a conscious decision to be constructive and to approach ownership with a positive attitude. When they go to owners' meetings, for example, they offer helpful comments and suggest solutions rather than just complaining, tearing down what someone else has done, or ridiculing others' positions. They exercise their rights with care and conscientiousness and with preparation.

They practice vigilance. They keep themselves informed about the business and are alert about developments that might affect it. They pay attention to their responsibilities as owners.

They find roles for themselves. Leaders inside the business often don't have time to take care of family matters as well. Outside owners play valuable roles in the family process, such as participating in or even heading the family council, chairing a committee, planning the next family meeting, or writing the company history. The family, as well as the business, needs leadership.

They make it a point to understand compensation. Effective owners know that their brothers and sisters working in the business deserve compensation as employees in addition to any dividends as shareholders. Compensation in family businesses is a frequent source of friction—largely because family members outside the business have little knowledge of what executives in their industry are paid. This information is available through industry associations and other sources and should be discussed openly at owners' meetings.

They appreciate the burden that family executives carry on behalf of the family. They understand the challenge of management and demonstrate a well-informed respect for managers and managing. They know that running the company, while it has its rewards, is very hard work, with long hours and heavy responsibilities.

They understand that owners are privileged. They recognize that having a family business brings many rewards that are not available to other people. They know that ownership is not an entitlement but a gift—

one that they will come to earn through their own stewardship.

They are self-aware. They are conscious of and honest with themselves about their own motives and desires, and avoid letting self-interest override the interests of others. They shun using their power as owners to get back at family members who may have hurt, angered, or disappointed them.

EXHIBIT 5 ████████████████████████████████████

Five Signs of Good Owners

- See themselves as stewards of the business.

- Consider the welfare of others—the business, the family, and other shareholders—as well as their own.

- Educate themselves about business ownership.

- Understand that ownership is a privilege.

- Try to add value to the business as an institution.

These attributes and behaviors comprise the effective ownership attitude—the attitude of stewardship that serves businesses and their owning families so well. While some are specific to owners who are not employed in the business, most can apply to all types of owners and can be adopted by anyone who has the will.

What You Will Inherit. . . And What You Won't

For more than 100 years, every generation of the Blethen family has embraced the concept of stewardship. The Blethens control *The Seattle Times* and several other newspapers. In a presentation at a meeting of the fifth generation, Frank Blethen, the fourth-generation chairman and publisher, offered his perspective to the younger family members. Here are excerpts:

- You inherit several things. First and foremost you will inherit the stewardship and the weighty responsibility that comes with it. It's the responsibility to perpetuate our quality, independent journalism and to pursue impactful, innovative community service. And, it's the responsibility to ensure we continue and enhance the business enterprise. And it's the responsibility to relentlessly pursue family harmony and inclusion.

- You will also inherit the right to participate as a Blethen family member and, if you choose, as a *Seattle Times* employee. Participation can take a variety of forms. Employment, career, senior management, governance. In every case, participation is encouraged but must be on a merit basis that maintains both family harmony and professional management. . . .

- You might inherit the right to dividends. However, your right to dividends is going to be based on the individual planning, choices and desires of your fathers in the fourth generation.

- So what do you not inherit? This is as important to understand as it is to understand what you inherit. You do not inherit liquidity and you do not inherit the right to sell the company.

- Liquidity is the term used for an investment or asset that you can quickly turn into personal cash. Businesses that don't operate like we do, on the basis of values and community service, or to perpetuate themselves, often do have liquidity as their key objective. But, not us. It's one of the things that distinguishes a public and private company from each other.

- In a private, values-based company, liquidity is often at odds with value fulfillment and long-term perpetuation of the business. It is very important you understand this as it gets to the heart of stewardship vs. ownership. Individual family members are responsible for their own personal finances.

- One of the things you will learn is that what you have, as a participant in a values-based family business, is something money simply can't buy. It is the opportunity to be part of a long journey in which the quality of the journey is paramount. You will learn that the relationships that you build with each other, as well as with non-family *Times* members who are committed to our values, will be among your absolute most valuable possessions.

A notion we mentioned in Chapter II bears repeating here. Even if you are not an actual owner, it pays to act like one. If you are the beneficiary of a trust or a young person who will inherit someday, you, your family, and the family business will benefit if you exhibit the behaviors and traits described above and if, the legal owners treat you with the respect they would give other owners. Acting like an owner, even though you don't have voting power, can be valuable to the whole group. It lets others know that you care about the business and the family and that you want to do what you can to support their mutual goals. When you have an ownership attitude, you become an asset and a resource to both.

V. Roles and Responsibilities: Owners, Directors, and Managers

Jeffrey doesn't like the way things are going. As the 17-percent owner of Woodruff Hardware, a wholesaler serving southeastern Pennsylvania, he thinks his opinion ought to count for more. A member of the family business' third generation, Jeffrey shares ownership equally with two brothers and three cousins. Only his brother, Phil, the CEO, and his cousin, Marissa, the CFO, work in the 80-employee company. Jeffrey is an internist with a busy practice and the other owners also have their own careers—one the chair of a high school English department; another, a nursing home administrator, and the third the manager of a conference center. Marissa and Phil are also the only owners on the board of directors.

Jeffrey was horrified recently to learn that on the company drawing board were some plans for aggressive expansion into Maryland, New Jersey, and Delaware. The plans were still just in an early-idea stage, to be sure, but Jeffrey thought the whole notion much too risky. "Are you crazy?" he said to Phil when he first heard about the idea. "Do you want to kill this company? Look at how much that's going to cost. You think I want to go the next five years without dividends?"

"But Marissa and I think expansion is the way to go," said Phil. "Mario's fine-tuning the proposal," he added, referring to the company's top non-family executive, the director of marketing and development. "When Marissa and I are satisfied that it's ready, we'll present it to the board. But it would sure help if we had your support."

"Not likely," Jeffrey muttered under his breath. Instead, he got on the phone to two of the company's three outside board members and urged them to argue against the idea. He also made a call to Mario. "Was this *your* idea?" he demanded. "What are you trying to do to me?" He called his other brother and cousins. They were surprised at the idea that the business might expand into other states, but a couple of them admitted they had not read some of the most recent information Phil and Marissa had sent to them. They had their own lives, after all. For their part, Phil and Marissa looked down a bit at their co-owners. . . and they have never really bothered to listen to their fellow owners' goals. These people, they reasoned, hadn't a clue about running a business.

Obviously, Jeffrey is confused about his role as an owner. He has overstepped bounds by lobbying board members and confronting an employee. But it also appears that the owners as a group don't understand their roles and responsibilities. Maybe they don't really recognize that they are part of a team that consists of owners, managers, and the board of directors. And perhaps no one has provided the leadership to help the group reach consensus on clearly articulated goals. Each group has a part to play in moving a family business forward. In the case of the Woodruff family (not their real name), two of the owners—Phil and Marissa—play multiple roles as owners, managers, and board members. Let's look at the role of each group.

EXHIBIT 6 ▬▬▬▬▬▬▬▬▬▬▬▬▬▬▬▬▬▬▬▬▬

Outside Owners Are Meddling When. . .

- They tell managers or employees what to do.
- They make decisions for the business on their own.
- They lobby individual board members.
- They violate policies the family has established.
- They naively ask questions or make comments that employees can misinterpret as commands.
- They complain that a spouse or a son or a daughter isn't getting adequate opportunities for promotions.

Owners: Values, Vision, Goals

Just what do good owners do? As pointed out earlier, owners have certain legal rights and powers. What we're interested in here, however, is owners' willingness to limit their own rights and do what's right, long-run, for others—other shareholders, the business itself as an institution, the family, the employees, and the community surrounding the business.

When owners are united, committed, and responsible, they make it possible for managers to do their jobs in an optimal way. Managers know where they stand, they know what the goals are, they know the owners will support them for the long term, and they know they can focus on the business instead of mediating or fearing shareholder disputes. In other words, a good ownership group is an outstanding asset to a family firm.

Ownerships first and foremost joint responsibility is to establish the values, vision, and goals that will guide the business and provide its framework.

A statement of values can include such treasured concepts as innova-

27

tion, trust, family, integrity, community, and openness. When family owners are clear about their agreed-upon values, they add richness and meaning and strength to the business' culture.

The owners' vision for the business is shaped by their values and encompasses two aspects:

(1) The nature of the business. Do the owners want a diversified, multi-business company or do they want to stay in one industry? Do they want to be local or regional, or do they want to be global? Do they want a business that welcomes family members as employees or that relies on non-family management or both?

(2) The structure of their ownership. The owning family must agree on and be clear about who can own shares and who can vote them. Some families want public ownership, others want private partners, and some want neither. Some families concentrate voting rights in trusts or general partners. Others eagerly distribute the shares quickly throughout the family and democ-ratize voting privileges.

Owners must also seek agreement on goals for the business that satisfy their own interests and secure their commitment and yet are reasonable for management to meet. Four areas for which owners must set goals are:

(1) **Growth.** For example, how fast do the owners want their business to grow and how large do they want it to become? Do they aim for rapid growth or seek growth at a steadier, more controlled pace? Do they favor growth in revenues or profitability?

(2) **Risk.** What risks are they willing to take as an ownership group? What strategy presents the most or least risk? What level of risk will be best for the business and the family?

(3) **Profitability.** What level of profitability do the owner's desire? What level is acceptable? What is unacceptable?

(4) **Liquidity.** The ownership group needs to give thought to liquidity—that is, how business assets can be converted to cash to fulfill the desires of individual owners who want to redeem their shares and how profits will be used. One of the owners' tasks is to develop a redemption policy, setting forth the condi-tions under which shares can be redeemed and the process for such redemption. Owners also establish the dividend payout ratio as a guide to the percentage of profit retained in the business and the percentage distributed to shareholders.

These four areas are, of course, interdependent. More of some means less of others—more growth usually means less liquidity. The trade-off a family chooses among its goals will reflect the owning family's values and vision for the business. One family may believe that the best way to assure owners' long-term commitment is through generous dividends and redemption opportunities. Another family may settle for smaller returns so that funds can be reinvested in growth or diversification that will eventually provide exciting careers for next-generation family members.

Once goals are established, ownership then should serve as a partner in strategy. This means helping management and the board to understand owner goals as a basis for developing the business's strategy and then embracing and supporting the strategy that is proposed by management and endorsed by the board.

Another key role of ownership is to assure excellent governance. It is a function of the owners to establish a process for choosing the board of directors, and they must be diligent about seeking, attracting, and electing the best directors they can find—directors who will help the owners achieve their goals. The owners themselves, as an owners council (see below) or shareholders group, can set an example of excellence in governance as they go about setting up their own decision-making process. If the process is seen as just or fair, owners' differences can be more readily accepted and worked through. If not, then unity and commitment are very much at risk.

On the family side, owners can lend encouragement and assistance in setting up a family council, family committees, family meetings, and the like. (Please see Family Business Leadership Series volume #8, *Family Business Governance: Maximizing Family and Business Potential.*)

Still another major responsibility of ownership is to address the issues that define its relationship with the business and to develop policies around them. Among the matters that owners need to address through policies are: interactions with management and directors, what information should be shared with owners, confidentiality, conflicts of interest, shareholder relations expenses, estate planning, share redemption, dividends, charitable giving, succession to governance roles, and board effectiveness. Some policies will be unique to the shareholders themselves (a shareholder relations expenses policy, for example), while others may overlap policies that affect the whole family, such as estate planning. [Please see *Developing Family Business Policies: Your Guide to the Future*, volume #11 in the Family Business Leadership Series.]

Sometimes older, larger family businesses, with many owners, address ownership issues and responsibilities through an ownership council. It is a representative group of owners, often major owners whose voting stock collectively comprises the majority of the voting shares. In other cases, the council members are elected by the family shareholders.

An ownership council may reserve the right to make certain decisions. It might get involved if there was an effort to sell all or part of the business or if the board and management are considering an acquisition exceeding a certain financial commitment. It might establish a limit on the company's debt-to-equity ratio or expect to be involved in any

EXHIBIT 7

Owners' Job Description

- It is the owners' responsibility to elect directors, and through their choice of directors, they exert their major influence on the company.

- Owners shall establish the values, vision, and goals that will guide the business and shall communicate these clearly and passionately to management and to the board of directors.

- The duty of ownership is to assure excellent governance, not only in their choice of directors but also in establishing a mechanism through which family ownership matters can be discussed and resolved. It is also ownership's duty to encourage or initiate the development of policies to guide the business and family in their relationship with each other.

- The owners shall work as partners with management and the board of directors, endorsing and supporting strategy and monitoring the business to assure that it reflects the values, vision, and goals that the owners have set forth.

- The owners shall regularly communicate with management, not only about financial progress but also about such matters as the business' role in the community and how it exemplifies the owners' values and goals.

---

dividend decisions that don't conform to the dividend policy.

One good reason for a business-owning family to have an ownership council is that it helps make distinctions between family issues, owner-ship issues, and management issues. The family council deals with family issues; the ownership council deals with ownership issues; the board of directors represents ownership in supporting management and holding it accountable; and the company's executives deal with management issues.

The Role of the Board

The primary responsibility of owners with voting shares is to elect the board of directors. The shareholders elect the directors and the board serves as the business' governing body. The board is charged with fiduciary responsibility for the company, representing the ownership in providing direction and oversight to the business. In effect, shareholders exert their control through their choice of directors.

The board's job is to represent the best interests of the owners as a whole. Therefore, good directors in family-owned businesses focus on understanding owners' values, vision, and goals and assure the business is operated to achieve owner goals consistent with their vision and values. If the owners have not been clear in these areas, then the directors' job is to encourage the family to speak on these matters with one voice.

The board has legal authority for the business and elects the company officers. It is the responsibility of the board to declare dividends when appropriate (that is, if the board believes funds are available after future operating and growth needs are taken into consideration).

A board fulfills its role in a variety of other ways as well, some of them very subtle. It offers advice and counsel to management, it endorses strategy, and it certifies, in a sense, that the activities of the business and management are consistent with the owners' values, vision, and goals of the owners. It will most likely help the family manage succession to the next generation of leaders and owners.

What Management Does

In the simplest terms, the role of managers is to develop and execute the business' strategy and to meet the expectations of the board and the owners through their leadership of the company. Managers should perform their duties in keeping with the values, vision, and goals that the owners propose and that the directors endorse and oversee. It is also the duty of management to keep the board and shareholders fully informed on the progress of the business, providing them with financial data and other information.

Helpful Hints

Owners, directors, managers, and board members can do much to assure that their partnership with one another is effective and harmonious. The following ideas should be helpful:

FOR OWNERS:

Speak with one voice. This is one of the most important things you can do. Have your meetings and your discussions, make decisions, and then let the board and management know what those decisions are. When you can't present a solid front, management feels insecure and uneasy, and spends too much of its energy trying to deal with owners as opposed to running the business.

Let managers do their jobs. Interference from owners undermines their ability to do their best for you.

Express your appreciation to managers. Take the time to say thanks. Honor with recognition those who serve you. But also richly reward key managers with pay, bonuses, and other forms of compensation, and by offering them opportunities to participate in profitable ventures.

Respect the chain of command. Deal only with top-level managers; don't go around them. Likewise, honor channels of communication.

Don't step outside your role. Unless you are a manager as well as an owner, don't expect to play a role in hiring or in telling managers what to do. Unless you are on the board, don't expect to have a voice at board meetings. And don't lobby individual board members. That puts them in a difficult position.

A few years ago, David E. Grant, a fourth-generation member of the Scotland-based scotch whiskey company, William Grant & Sons, Inc., described the owners' changing role over the years. "A family firm starts out as owner-managed," he said. As a business develops, the overlap between business and management is progressively reduced. "Eventually the board emerges as a discrete third circle. By next year at William Grant & Sons, the linkage from the family to the management will be only through the board."

FOR BOARD MEMBERS:

This advice is of particular relevance to board members from outside the family:

Represent the family as a whole, not a particular individual. Some owners may put pressure on you to present their point of view. Resist the pressure. Try to do what's best for the business so that the whole family will benefit.

Avoid arbitrating family problems. Make it clear that's not your role or expertise.

Avoid conflicts of interest. Maintain a cordial relationship with all owners and managers but resist getting too chummy with any of them.

FOR MANAGERS:

Be "transparent." Be open about and accountable for everything that you do.

Provide information. Keep all owners up to speed on what is going on in the company. This builds trust and wins their support.

Respect all owners. Even if you are an owner yourself, it's helpful to be caring of owners outside the business. They may not know as much as you do about the business, but it's part of your job to keep them committed and supportive.

We like a metaphor used by family business consultant, Ivan Lansberg, to explain the difference between owners and managers: Imagine that the business is a 747. What the family owners are responsible for is how the plane is used. Will it carry passengers? Cargo? Drugs? War material? The family chooses the airplane's use but it does not fly the plane. It hires a pilot (or manager) to fly the plane and determine the flight plan, and other crew members to attend to other needs. The crew then executes the plane's mission. The family owners stay out of the cockpit. They don't serve drinks or collect the trash. They let the pilot and crew do their jobs.

The six owners of Woodruff Hardware, at the beginning of this chapter, could have benefited from much of what has been presented here. It seems likely that several of the Woodruffs are confused or indifferent about their roles as owners. It's clear that they haven't formed any consensus around values, vision, and goals. They do not speak with one voice. But they have a great opportunity now, if only they will take advantage of it.

VI. Preparing and Nurturing Good Owners

"I don't get it," said Alan, the 20-year-old grandson of the founder of a substantial distribution business. Although not active in the business, he owns a small stake in it and he regularly attended family meetings. He was talking with a cousin during a break. As a philosophy major in college, he felt that he was headed in professional directions the opposite of business.

"A couple of years ago, we wrote and adopted a noble-sounding family mission statement," he said. But we've spent the last two hours talking about inventory turns. How boring! What do they have to do with our family mission or our family relationships?"

"Why don't you ask that question when we reconvene?" challenged the cousin.

Before the break, the six family members who held executive positions in the company sat before 23 relatives, all owners. They had pointed out slightly improved profitability resulting from a healthy increase in volume, achieved in part through improving average inventory turns from 6.8 to 7.2 times per year, despite the fact that it is taking longer to collect receivables.

"Any questions on the report?" asked the second-generation CEO.

Alan's hand shot up. "What does increasing inventory turns have to do with our family's mission statement?"

The room was quiet. "That's a great question," the CEO responded. "Who wants to answer?"

Tentatively, one family member spoke up: "With more inventory turns, we sell more stuff and make more money. And then we can use the money to do good things."

"Yeah," added another. "In our mission statement, we promise to be good stewards of resources entrusted to our care. If inventory is turning faster, then things are sitting around less and we are doing a better job of stewardship."

"Good answers," said the CEO. "But how can we improve inventory turns?"

"Smarter buying," "knowing what our customers want," "the willingness to invest in technology, facilities, and training that permit continuous improvement," came some answers.

"Let me summarize what I've heard," offered the CEO. "Our mission statement speaks of family unity and opportunity. It describes the benefits of actively owning and managing a business. It states that we accept responsibility for the stewardship of our resources and for providing stable, meaningful employment. It says that we expect our enterprises to be managed in a way that produces a better-than-average return on our investment. And it says we'll use some of the profits we earn toward the improvement of our community and environment."

While inventory turns sounded mundane, the CEO said, "I think we can see that it relates to every aspect of our family's mission. Alan, thank you for your question."

Alan had never thought of business as containing so much philosophy. And he had never considered philosophy to be of much relevance to practical matters like inventory turns.

"I think I'm beginning to get it," he said.

Passing on the Legacy of Effective Ownership

This little story offers a rich example of how education and preparation for business ownership might occur in a caring family. First, there is Alan, the confused young owner, trying to figure out why something as "boring" as inventory turns has anything to do with the noble goals the family has set out for itself in its mission statement. Alan asks his question in the family meeting, essentially taking a step to educate himself.

Others in the group listen to Alan's question and treat him with respect as they suggest some answers. There's a sense in the group that Alan is not the only one who doesn't know the answer to his question and that it is worth discussing.

Led by the CEO, the group reviews the family's mission statement and looks at how it relates to the inventory turns. In so doing, the members are reminding themselves of what the family stands for and how it uses the business to meet its goals. Before long, Alan begins to see the connection between inventory turns and goals like providing employment and improving the community.

One of the secrets to the longevity of the century-old businesses we mentioned earlier is that they have passed to each succeeding generation the understanding of *how* to be good owners.

Responsible ownership of a family business doesn't come naturally. It has to be learned—just as a person has to learn responsible ownership of an automobile (you have to drive it properly and keep it well-maintained) or a house (you have to clean it and paint it and keep it in good repair).

Unfortunately, when it comes to teaching the next generation about effective business ownership, many families just leave it to chance.

Chance generally doesn't work very well, and many of these same families end up searching for ways to protect the business *from* the owners because the owners haven't developed any understanding of their responsibilities.

At its best, the preparation of family members for effective ownership involves (1) a family that is committed to nurturing their development as owners and (2) potential or new owners who have pledged themselves to being good owners and have committed themselves to learning how. The rest of this chapter assumes that you are part of a family that wants to know more about how to bring along the next generation of owners, or that you yourself are an owner or a future owner who wants to learn the fundamentals of effective ownership.

Educating the Next Generation for Ownership

EXHIBIT 8 ▰▰▰▰▰▰▰▰▰▰▰▰▰▰▰▰

Benefits of Being an Educated Owner

- You become worthy of what you own. You "earn" ownership by helping to preserve and build the business for the next generation.

- You gain credibility and your opinion is more respected.

- You enjoy an opportunity to contribute to a purpose larger than yourself.

- You feel more connected to the business and the family.

- You can become active in protecting and enhancing the asset that you own.

The best way to protect the future of the business and enhance its continuity in the family is to prepare the next generation of owners for their roles and responsibilities. Family business leaders—and those of us who advise business-owning families—spend a great deal of time on the training and development of the next generation of managers and leaders within the business. But training and developing the future owners, whether or not they work inside the business, is equally important.

As we have seen in earlier chapters, knowledgeable, sensitive owners provide their management with the support it needs to move a business forward. They find constructive ways to resolve conflicts and differences. They work to balance the needs of the business and the family. They help assure that the business exemplifies the values of the family. Their positive attitudes and clearly articulated values and commitment to the welfare of others enhance the harmony of the family.

Uneducated, uncaring or selfish owners, however, can destroy a business and do long-lasting harm to a family. Not understanding what the business requires to survive and prosper, they may be concerned primarily about receiving dividends and supporting their own lifestyles. At their worst, they kill the goose that lays the golden eggs, and they create irreparable ill feeling in the family.

If you are a shareholder who is concerned about preparing the next generation for effective ownership, here are some steps you can take:

Be a good owner yourself. Adopt an ownership attitude (see Chapter IV) and set an example that other family members can aspire to. Children learn by example, but so do adults. Understand that the first lesson young people learn about good ownership comes from being part of a family that takes meaning and value and satisfaction from being owners of a business.

Concentrate on developing good values, morals, and ethics in children. Good, responsible, effective ownership is rooted in values and ethics. Establish these and good ownership is likely to follow.

Instill stewardship. Convey to future shareholders that ownership means taking care of a business, just as they were taught to take care of their toys when they were children. It's not about power or control.

Begin when the kids are young. In education, you introduce new information a little at a time, as the youngster is able to absorb and understand it. Ownership education is no different. As you introduce information, take the opportunity to make your own values clear and reinforce the lessons of values and ethics. Expose children to the business at an early age. Provide them with early, positive experiences in the business. Try to convey that the business not only provides the family with an enjoyable lifestyle, but that it also requires hard work and discipline.

Responsible ownership of a family business doesn't come naturally. It has to be learned.

Understand the power of the dinner table. Most of the lessons young people will learn about responsible ownership will come to them informally—at the dinner table, in the car, at your side on a stroll through the business, during a company picnic. Look for opportunities to present lessons in a fun, informal way. One son recalls how his father, a clothing wholesaler, used to stop at his customers' stores in small towns on family vacations. "They seemed happy to see us. They greeted us in a very gracious way, sometimes taking us to their houses for a meal." Sometimes the father would come away from these visits with an order or cash collected on account. And one time, on a drive through a town square full of people when the son was about 11, his dad said, "I bet our underwear's on every butt in this town."

Says the son: "I learned more about distribution from that comment than I ever did from any class in business school. And I began to understand that what we did was help these people get their clothes, and that was important, and that we were part of this big network of folks that were out there who were engaged in this sort of thing. I thought it was pretty cool. If you had sat me down and lectured me on the business, I would have gone to sleep."

Don't shield children from knowledge, good or bad. When there's a crisis or when something wonderful happens use the event as an opportunity to help them understand the business. Talk about what happened and why it's important and how the resulting decisions were made and—most important—the values that went into the decisions.

Take the mystery out of ownership. Ownership should not be seen as rites of passage to adulthood but as something that is part of the essence of being in a business-owning family. Be transparent and open about it. Don't be secretive about who owns stock. Answer young people's questions. Invite them to shareholder meetings, even if they're not yet shareholders.

Some of the tools families can use to educate present and future shareholders about ownership are:

Family meetings. Plan to include educational components that center around how to be a good owner. The family attorney, for example, can be invited to help shareholders understand their legal rights and responsibilities. A knowledgeable non-family executive can talk about the company's strategy and how it relates to the family's goals.

Financial statements. Use profit-and-loss statements, balance sheets, and other financial reports as opportunities for education. Distribute them and discuss them (see Exhibit 9). Relate them to the goals and values of the family, as Alan's elders did in discussing inventory turns.

Meetings of sibling or cousin teams. These peer groups can come together regularly to discuss ownership as it relates to them, share their own experiences, and learn from one another.

Tutoring sessions. Some families ask their CFO or outside accountant to conduct tutoring sessions to help family members learn how to understand and use financial statements. The same technique can be used for other subject matter. The marketing chief could hold a session on the company's marketing initiatives or an attorney could help owners better understand shareholder agreements. You might also consider bringing in a panel of shareholders from other well-run family businesses to talk about how they handle their responsibilities as owners.

Communication and information sharing. Newsletters, letters from the CEO, annual shareholders' meetings, and even e-mail are all tools that can be used to educate owners. They are also essential factors in building and maintaining trust among shareholders.

Educating Yourself for Ownership

There are many reasons why it's important to prepare yourself as an owner, but one of the most important ones is very personal: You most likely have or will come into ownership by virtue of inheritance. You may feel like you didn't earn what you own or contribute to it. As a result, you may be having feelings of unworthiness. After all, this was a privilege you received by birthright or as a result of the generosity of someone else.

When you prepare yourself to be a good owner, you are creating the opportunity for yourself to contribute. You are finding the way to earn what you own by being a good steward of it—preserving and building it for the next generation, for employees, and for the community.

Education for ownership isn't something you do once, and then it's done. It's a continuing, lifetime activity.

Another critical reason for preparing yourself is that **the more knowledgeable and trustworthy you are, the more your opinion will be respected and the more effective you can be as an owner.**

If all the reasons stated weren't enough, here are some additional reasons for preparing yourself for ownership: You will get more satisfaction and enjoyment from family business ownership when you are involved in it, committed to it, and knowledgeable about it. Being an effective owner enables you to be active in protecting and enhancing the asset that you own. You will enjoy an opportunity to contribute to a purpose larger than yourself, something that most human beings yearn for. And, being an active, participating owner means that you will become more involved in the family and just plain have more fun.

Ideally, your family will have provided you with preparation for ownership responsibilities. But that is all too often not the case and, as we have suggested, if there are no mechanisms in place in the family or the business to prepare family members for ownership, you will have to take on the responsibility of preparing yourself.

Be assured: It's never too late. Education for ownership isn't just for the young. If you have been an owner for a long time but have been confused about or even frightened by the prospect of the responsibilities of ownership, you can benefit from preparation. Katharine Graham, who was mentioned earlier in this book, became the owner of The Washington Post Co. with her husband at the age of 31, but her real education as an owner began 15 years later on her husband's death.

Preparation means more than just gaining knowledge. It also—and more importantly—means having the ownership attitude discussed in Chapter IV. We encourage you to read that chapter again and again. **The first step toward preparing yourself is to make a commitment to becoming a good owner or transforming yourself into one. In other words, you pledge yourself to be an effective steward of the asset that you own.** You can have all the knowledge in the world or be as smart as they come and still be a lousy owner.

Pledge yourself to be an effective steward of the asset that you own.

Good ownership requires practical knowledge, wisdom, and character, all of which over time are enriched by experience.

That said, however, there are some fundamental things you need to know and understand to be a good owner. These include:

—**How to read financial statements** and an understanding of measurement criteria used to monitor a business' progress (those inventory turns again!). You will want to understand such items as balance sheets (statements showing the financial position of a company at a given point in time), income statements (reports that show a company's revenues, expenses, and profits over a period of time), and cash flow analyses (which show the movement of cash into and out of the company)(see exhibit 9). We suggest some resources for this kind of knowledge in the section, "Suggested Readings and Resources, on page 61.''

—**The basics of the family's business and the industry it's in.** Each industry, whether it's commercial landscaping, making movies, or meat processing has its own challenges. You can obtain information about your industry from industry or trade associations. Look, also, for relevant business histories and biographical books. If you're in the newspaper business, for example, *Personal History,* the book by Katharine Graham

EXHIBIT 9 ■■■■■■■■■■■■■■■■■■■■■■■■■■

How's Business

How's business? That's a question to which every business owner wants to know the answer. That answer is often compli-cated—but understanding financial statements including balance sheets (see example) and "P&Ls" (profit and loss state-ments)(see example) often provide a pretty good picture of how businesses are performing.

Many family business financial statements contain idiosyn-crasies related to the specific circumstances or industry of the business. That's why financial statements are reviewed, explained and discussed by top management at board or share-holders meetings.

Balance sheets and P&Ls are both snapshots. At a particular point in time, the balance sheet lists the company's assets (all things owned by the business including money owed to the business) and liabilities (debts and other obligations). It also subtracts liabilities from assets indicating the business's "book value" or "shareholder's equity". Most business owners hope to increase the value of their business so watching the trend related to book value (up or down) and how fast the company is growing (10 to 20 percent annually is often a healthy goal but growth rate is a variable related to corporate strategy), are important indicators of company well being. Another impor-tant indicator is the "debt-to-equity ratio". Dividing long-term debt by shareholders' equity indicates the company's ability to pay back its liabilities or to access more debt to invest in pursuing its strategy. A 1:1 debt to equity ratio, for example, means that the business has equal amounts of debt and equity that might be considered overly aggressive or risky by some family businesses. The company's board should have a policy concerning the acceptable debt-to-equity ratio and exceeding that ratio may be cause for concern.

The profit and loss statement reveals the company's revenue or gross income, expenses, and net income or profit (revenue minus expenses). Generally, businesses like revenue to increase, expenses to increase more slowly than revenue, and net income increase as well. Since the P&L usually lists many specific expenses, various expenses can also be tracked as management may target specific costs for reduction (interest, salaries, insurance or entertainment might be examples). Cost of goods sold is often separated from "general and administrative" (G&A) expenses. Profit as a percent of sales is often a focus but varies widely in different industries.

An important indicator of business health takes the net revenues from the P&L and divides it by the shareholders' equity figure from the balance sheet. The result is called "return on investment" or "R.O.I.". The R.O.I. is stated as a percentage. A 7% R.O.I. would mean that shareholder's return on investment would be similar to that achieved by investing in long-term secure bonds. Since being in business exposes shareholders to risk, generally speaking their returns should be higher than what they would expect to earn from less risky investments like government bonds or insured savings accounts. Depending on the business, the industry, the state of the economy and many other factors, most business owners would consider good an average annual return to be in the 15-25% range.

---

of the *Washington Post* mentioned earlier, and *The Trust*, by Susan E. Tifft and Alex S. Jones (Little, Brown, 1999) a book about the family behind *The New York Times*, are excellent choices. If you're in the candy business, take a look at *The Emperors of Chocolate*, by Joel Glenn Brenner (Random House, 1999), about the Mars and Hershey companies.
   —**What the family's values are and how these relate to or are reflected by the business.** Does your family prize education, a certain religion, charity, equal opportunity for all? You already know what your family's values are because you grew up with them. What you need to learn now—by attending family meetings and shareholder meetings and by asking questions of older family members—is how those values play out in the business.
   —**What the family's goals are and how to evaluate the company's progress toward those goals.** Again, you can learn more about family goals and even help shape them by participating in family meetings and other family events. Ask what tools the family uses to measure the company's success in helping the family meet its goals. If a family goal is to help immigrant families in the community, for example, ask what

SMALL FAMBIZ
BALANCE SHEET
as of December 31, 2000

Assets

Current Assets

Cash		$ 4,000
Marketable Securities		75,000
Accounts Receivable	$ 279,000	
Less: Allowance for Doubtful Accounts	8,000	271,000
Notes Receivable		122,000
Inventory		156,000
Prepaid Expenses		16,000
Total Current Assets		**$ 644,000**

Fixed Assets

Store Equipment	$ 271,000	
Less: Accumulated Depreciation	115,000	$ 156,000
Furniture and Fixtures	$ 79,000	
Less: Accumulated Depreciation	24,000	55,000
Total Fixed Assets		**$ 211,000**

Intangible Assets

Copyrights	$ 5,000	
Total Intangible Assets		5,000
Total Asset		**$ 860,000**

Liabilities and Owners' Equity

Current Liabilities

Accounts Payable	$ 241,000	
Current Installments of Long Term Debt	115,000	
Accrued Expenses	27,000	
Income Taxes Payable	36,000	
Total Current Liabilities		**$ 419,000**

Long Term Liabilities

Long-Term Notes Payable	$ 230,000	
Total Long-Term Liabilites		$ 230,000
Total Liabilities		**$ 649,000**

Owners' Equity

Common Stock	$ 10,000	
Retained Earnings	201,000	
Total Owners' Equity		**$ 211,000**
Total Liabilities and Owners' Equity		**$ 860,000**

SMALL FAMBIZ
INCOME STATEMENT
For the Year Ended December 31, 2000

Revenues

Gross Sales		$1,300,000	
Less: Sales Returns and Allowances		48,000	
Net Sales			**$1,252,000**

Costs of Goods Sold

Beginning Inventory		$ 265,000	
Purchases during Year	$550,000		
Less: Purchase Discounts	55,000		
Net Purchases		495,000	
Cost of Goods Available for Sale		$ 760,000	
Less: Ending Inventory, Dec. 31		216,000	
Cost of Goods Sold			**$ 544,000**

Gross Profit   **$ 708,000**

Operating Expenses

Selling Expenses

Sales Salaries and Commissions	$251,000		
Advertising	116,000		
Depreciation: Store Equipment	15,000		
Miscellaneous Selling Expenses	33,000		
Total Selling Expenses		$ 415,000	

General and Admin Expenses

Office Salaries	$155,000		
Rent	30,000		
Office Supplies	18,000		
Depreciation: Office Equipment	13,000		
Misc. Gen'l Expense	12,000		
Total General Expenses		$ 228,000	

Total Expenses	**$ 643,000**
Net Income Before Taxes	65,000
Less: Income Taxes	11,250
Net Income	**$ 53,750**

the company has done and is doing to support this goal. Is it hiring immigrant workers or making it possible for them to attend classes in English as a second language?

—**What the business' culture is and how owners can contribute to it.** Corporate culture refers to the environment within a company. It consists of the company's "personality," the way things are done in the company, its ethics and values, its goals, its traditions, and the spirit it engenders. Some companies are hard driving, sales-oriented enterprises. Others appear to be fun loving but socially concerned. Still others, many high-technology companies among them, emphasize innovation and informality. A family business leader, backed by the family owners, shapes the culture of a family firm.

—**The concept of strategy and what the strategy of your business is.** Strategy refers to a company's plan of action, developed with respect to such factors as the environment in which a company operates, market conditions, customer wants and needs, anticipated trends, changes in technology, and the company's own strengths and weaknesses. Your family business might choose among such strategies as moving into new geographic markets, acquiring other businesses, introducing new products or services, and applying new technology to improve an existing service.

—**The tradeoffs of business growth versus liquidity and dividends.** Dividends that are too high or untimely liquidity demands can cripple a business by draining needed capital. Lack of dividends or liquidity on the other hand can diminish shareholder support for the business.

—**The challenges of management and the difficulties of being a director or a manager.** If you have watched the television show, "Who Wants To Be a Millionaire?," you know how often new contestants comment on the difficulty of being in the "hot seat." It looks so easy when you're just watching it on TV! So it is with being a director or a manager. These are hard jobs. Managers must put in long hours, think incisively, cope with difficult personnel issues, inspire others to give their best performance, deal with several layers of government, manage crises, and much more. Directors must make difficult decisions, bear fiduciary responsibility, and offer wise guidance.

—**The principles of family business governance,** including how a family council, a board of directors, and management all work to guide the family and the business.

—**Self-awareness and self-knowledge.** Understand how your values, preferences, and actions affect others simply *because* you are an owner. (You casually mention to the facilities manager that you like red walls and you may arrive at the business a few days later to find all the office walls painted red.) It's also important to understand your own motivations and how they affect your behavior and decisions.

—**Your legal rights and responsibilities as an owner**— For example, do you have voting rights? How does being a minority shareholder affect your rights? (See Chapter II for a more detailed discussion.)

—**An understanding of business compensation in your industry**— such as salary, bonuses, and benefits. Remember that family managers, even if they are owners, are entitled to compensation for their work just as they would be if they were employed in a company outside the family business. Industry groups are a good source of compensation information.

Where else can you go to learn what you need to know as an owner? Here are some helpful ideas:

Ask for help. Express your desire to learn to someone in the family who is in a position to appreciate your attitude and to facilitate your learning process. This could be a leader in the business or a family leader retired from the business. Perhaps this individual or someone else—a trusted non-family executive, for example—would be willing to serve as your mentor.

Like Alan did at the beginning of this chapter, screw up your courage and ask some questions at family or shareholder meetings.

Read, read, read. Libraries and bookstores offer countless books on business, ranging from how to read financial statements to strategic planning. Some self-improvement or psychology books may also be helpful in gaining self-understanding. Periodicals such as *The Wall Street Journal, Harvard Business Review,* and the major business magazines deliver general business knowledge in a lively, readable way. Trade journals offer information about specific industries. And, of course, today there are countless World Wide Web sites that can expand your business knowledge. In addition, our monthly newsletter, The *Family Business Advisor* (www.efamilybusiness.com), is filled with articles on family business topics, including many on ownership issues.

Read, read, read some more. As an owner, you should be getting financial statements and other reports from management—perhaps quarterly reports, newsletters, and house organs. Read them to gain an understanding of how the business works and to keep up on current developments.

Attend meetings. Make it a point to be present at shareholders meetings and family meetings. Ask if you can be invited to board meetings from time to time as part of your on-going education process. Some families rotate some of the board seats, giving different shareholders the opportunity to serve and to learn more about the business.

Involve yourself. Volunteer to chair or serve on a family or ownership committee. Offer to set up the educational sessions at the next family meeting (a great opportunity to include some ownership education!), to serve as the family business archivist or historian or to draft a family mission statement.

Attend seminars and courses. Local colleges, investment companies, the U.S. Small Business Administration, Chambers of Commerce and other organizations offer a variety of programs that can be helpful. Scores of universities hold family business education programs. (Contact us at 800-551-0633 for information on a program near you.)

Obviously, there is much that a senior generation of shareholders can do to prepare the next generation for effective family business ownership. There is also much that shareholders and future shareholders can do to prepare themselves.

In any case, preparation for ownership is of vital concern to a family business. Succession and estate planning get lots of attention as the critical keys to family business continuity, but the preparation of committed, caring, knowledgeable owners is even more important.

Education for ownership isn't something you do once, and then it's done. It's a continuing, lifetime activity. There is always something new to learn, either about the business, about the family, or about improving one's competency as an owner. And that never-ending learning is part of what makes being an owner exciting and enjoyable.

VII. Owners By Choice

As we mentioned earlier, except for business founders, most family business owners don't choose to become owners. Ownership usually comes to them via inheritance or as a gift.

It is critically important, however, that *remaining* an owner be a matter of choice. A family business deserves owners who *want* to be owners, not owners who are forced to be. Nothing could be worse for a business than having uncommitted, unhappy owners. Yet many miserable shareholders continue as owners because the price of not being one is just too high

A family business deserves owners who want to be owners, not owners who are forced to be.

or because they see no way out. And in many family businesses, there isn't one.

Ownership as a Trap

Owners who want to be owners do so for a variety of reasons. They say: "Being an owner helps me feel connected to the family." "This is part of my legacy." "I'm a steward, too, and it's part of my responsibility to carry this business on." or, "I like the financial returns." Some also think that ownership offers them unofficial rights, such as the right to employment in the business or a seat on the board. Obviously, owners don't want to give up what they perceive as benefits.

Nevertheless, some of what may seem to be benefits can be traps. It's not healthy, for example, when ownership is the only thing or the main thing that makes an individual feel connected to the family. When asked why they don't sell their stock, some people say, "Because that would cut me off from the family." So they stay owners when they would rather not.

Unofficial entitlements, such as providing owners with employment or the prestige of being on the board or other perks just because they are owners, are inappropriate and something we discourage. They're not good for the business, and probably not good for the family either.

Staying an owner because you like the dividends is fine for an investor, but it doesn't qualify you as a good and effective family business owner. Better perhaps to sell your shares to a family member who would really care about being an owner and invest your proceeds somewhere else.

Providing an Exit

We encourage business-owning families to provide shareholders with the opportunity to make a "graceful exit" from ownership. The only way to make ownership truly voluntary is to give owners the option of getting out, and that requires the family to have some kind of redemption policy.

Many families avoid creating redemption policies under the questionable notion that they want owners to stay owners forever. They fear the harm that can come to a business when the demands for redemption that are placed on it at any one time become too great for it to handle.

That's a legitimate fear, but it's one that can be managed through a carefully crafted policy that balances the needs of people who want to cash in their shares with the needs of the business for capital. Such a policy is likely to state that redemption CAN occur, but that it can only occur under certain circumstances—such as when a given amount of money is available. It might specify that redemption can occur when capitalization exceeds a certain amount, or provide that a certain percentage of profit will be set aside each year in a pool that will be available for redemptions.

Creating a redemption policy is not a do-it-yourself project. Such policies are complicated from the perspective of tax and securities law, and they get you and other owners into discussions of difficult issues, such as the value of shares, shareholder or buy-sell agreements, and the like. You will need the help of your lawyer and your accountant in drafting a redemption policy. And again, two other volumes in the Family Business Leadership Series will be helpful: #7, *Financing Transitions: Managing Capital and Liquidity in the Family Business*, and #11, *Developing Family Business Policies: Your Guide to the Future.* The latter, for example, offers a detailed discussion of shareholder agreements.

Unhappy Owners

What if you're an owner who is unhappy with the way the business is being managed? Well, there are "best practices" that unhappy owners can follow.

One case of ownership disaffection became very public several years ago when unhappy minority family owners pushed for change at Dow Jones. The minority owners went to great effort to be responsible, even seeking advice from the famous financial guru, Warren Buffett. But they also created a stir that was widely covered in the business press, and some would disagree that that was the right thing to do.

We suggest to **unhappy owners** that they **are acting responsibly when they (1) are educated about the issues on which they disagree; (2) put the collective interest ahead of their individual interest; and**

(3) go through proper channels, bringing up issues with the family council or council of elders, and speaking up at shareholders' meetings. It can be damaging to the family and to the business to air one's disaffection to the media in hopes of bringing about change, and we don't advise it.

What if, from your point of view, you've done all the right and responsible things and there is no change? First, you can attempt to pull together a significant group of owners who share your views and express them to the Board of Directors. As a last resort, you can sell your stock. As any good owner knows, it will be hard to stay effective as an owner of a business when you are so dismayed with the way it is being run. Selling when you really want to be a good owner, however, is a very difficult choice to make.

"Emotional" Liquidity

A business-owning family needs not only to provide opportunities for financial liquidity for owners but also to provide them with "emotional" liquidity. By that, we mean families ought not confuse ownership of the business with membership in the family. When an individual chooses not to be an owner any longer, he should not be made to feel that he's a disgrace to the family, that he is betraying others, or that Great Grandfather is turning over in his grave. A graceful exit means a family member should be able to depart ownership with dignity and without being judged by others. It also means assuring people that, although they are no longer a part of the business, they are still an important, valued, and welcome part of the family.

> *Families ought not confuse ownership of the business with membership in the family.*

A side benefit of providing owners with opportunities for exit is that doing so contributes to their independence. It enables them to make important decisions about their own lives.

The most important benefit to the business, however, is that it helps assure a caring, active, committed ownership group. It provides an opportunity for weeding out indifferent or unhappy owners and replacing them with owners who will give the business the support it needs to prosper.

VIII. Managing the Insider-Outsider Dilemmas

Every family business has "insiders" and "outsiders": Owners who work in the business and owners who don't; family members who own shares and family members who don't; married couples where one spouse is an owner and the other is not; owners with voting stock and owners with non-voting stock or family members whose shares are held in trust; majority owners and minority shareholders.

The perceptions of each group about the other can breed a resentment that can be destructive to the effectiveness of the ownership group as a whole or harmful to personal relationships in the family. When owners recognize those perceptions, they can take steps to prevent or mitigate needless conflict. Let's begin with one of the most pervasive pairings: owners who work inside the business and those who don't.

EXHIBIT 10

Insiders and Outsiders: Some Differences

Owners INSIDE the Business:	Owners OUTSIDE the Business:
■ Have more access to knowledge and information.	■ Have less access to knowledge and information.
■ Are so steeped in the business they don't recognize what others don't know.	■ Want to feel more connected to the business.
■ Have power and status and can make important decisions.	■ May be confused and overwhelmed by the responsibilities of ownership.
■ Work hard and carry a heavy burden.	■ Often feel disrespected by owner/managers.
■ May view owners outside the business as parasites.	■ May suspect that owner/managers receive inflated salaries and perks.

Inside Owners Versus Outside Owners

Owner/managers have much more access to knowledge about the business than do their outside counterparts. They are so imbued in the business that they usually can't even recognize what others don't know and what it would take for them to understand. Owner/managers have power. They can make important decisions. They often have status in the business, in the family, and in the community. Outside owners, by contrast, lack easy access to information about the business. They don't feel as connected to the business as the insiders and, as a result, often experience less "psychic income" from it. If they don't live in the community where the business is located, they may feel even more disconnected. They may be jealous of the status and power of the insiders.

These differences lead to friction. Sometimes owners who work inside the company as managers take a dim view of owners who aren't employed in the business. The insiders may see the outsiders as parasites, while they view themselves as burdened with long hours and heavy responsibility. "Why should I be working so hard just so she can collect a dividend?" the insider may wonder.

Insiders also may, at least silently, deride the outsiders for their ignorance of the business or lack of knowledge of the industry. They get angry at the outsiders' seeming obsession with dividends or liquidity when, they think, everybody should know that dividends and redemptions would drain the business of needed capital.

In fact, insiders may fear outside owners, wishing they would just go away because the outsiders put pressure on owner/managers and make their lives more difficult. In some inside owners' eyes, the outsiders are the enemy.

For their part, outside shareholders may see the insiders as over-privileged. The outsider's lament goes something like this:

> There they are, my cousins, the prestigious executives. They sit on other people's boards and get a lot of glowing attention in the community. They get fat salaries and god-knows-what perks.

> They never tell me what's going on. I can't remember the last time they sent out any information that meant anything to me. Seems to me they're trying to cover up what they're doing. The annual shareholders meetings? They're just a joke. The insiders just talk to each other and don't say anything I can understand. Except that all the time they're wailing about how little money is available and how what there is has to be plowed back into the company, and how we should not expect any dividends anytime soon. They ask us to tighten our belts. Meanwhile, they're driving fancy cars and taking trips. I just don't trust them anymore.

Either side could go on and on about the other with a litany of complaints. And, unfortunately, sometimes, there's truth in the complaints. How to prevent or resolve such dilemmas? The first and most powerful step is to challenge your assumptions about the other side and to treat all owners with respect. Maybe your assumptions about the others are simply wrong.

This is especially true of insiders, who tend not to treat outsiders as respectfully as they should. The outsiders pick up on that quickly and resentment builds.

Below are some other steps owners can take.

OWNER/MANAGERS SHOULD:

Accept all owners. Understand that they have real needs to understand and to deal with the responsibilities of ownership and that they can contribute to the welfare of the business.

Be open about and accountable for what you do. Share information about what's being spent on initiatives to develop the business for the future. Communicate with all owners about expenses, and help outside owners understand what's appropriate and necessary. Be open about salaries and perks and provide evidence that they fall within industry practices.

Strive to create a "heirloom effect" for the non-employed owners. Help them see that the business that they own is precious. Ways to do this include creating good will for them in the community, honoring or creating traditions that focus on purpose or meaning, providing opportunities for them to see things about the company that will make them proud, or helping them meet people they will find interesting to know. These and other techniques help outside owners feel more connected to the business and increase their sense of "psychic reward."

Provide adequate information. Make sure it is in a form that all shareholders can understand.

Be honest. Don't give a false picture of the company just so you can manipulate other owners or hold down dividends.

Be a good communicator. This means more than providing financial or technical data. It means telling the story of the company's progress, with heart and enthusiasm. You might do this through meetings, monthly CEO newsletters, and even one-on-one conversations.

Listen. Pay attention to the concerns of other shareholders and address them respectfully. Listen to their ideas—one might be absolutely terrific for the company.

Be trustworthy. Do what you say you'll do. Extend trust to other shareholders.

Be an educator. It's true—outside shareholders probably don't know as much as you do about the business or about ownership. An important part of your job is to educate them. Think of it as "investor relations." Be VERY patient. Some shareholders are incredibly timid about business

EXHIBIT #11 ███████████████████████████████████

T-R-U-S-T—Five Ways To Build It

T — Teach your owners about how the business operates and what it means to be an owner.

R — Respect your owners, and understand the power of their potential contributions. See them as an asset.

U — Utilize input from your owners.

S — Share information with them.

T — Trust your owners and be trustworthy. Do what you say you will do.

---

and financial matters. Try to appreciate that, for them, talking about business and money may be as difficult as talking about death. You may need to take very small steps with them.

Be sensitive about power and status. Share credit with the family as a whole as often as you can; don't take all the credit yourself.

Consider buying out the outsiders. When your feelings about the outsiders are so negative that you can only think of them as parasites, some changes need to be made. You can either change your attitude about them or buy them out, and often buying them out is the more realistic choice.

Note that many of the above ideas are just as important for non-family managers with no ownership as they are for family owner/managers. Whether family or non-family, wise managers respect all owners, feel it is their duty to educate owners, are honest and open, and work to create the "heirloom effect." They know that there may be some risks involved in inviting outside owners to contribute to the business. But even if they wish owners would go away so their jobs would be more simple, they also know that ignoring owners is likely to backfire and make their own lives harder, not easier.

FOR OUTSIDE OWNERS:

Take a caring interest in the business. Commit yourself to the continuity and success of the asset you own and demonstrate that commitment to the inside owners. Focus on the welfare of others and on what's good for the business.

Understand and respect the challenges of management. Learn more about what your relatives actually DO in the business. Express appreciation for their hard work.

Educate yourself. Chances are, you don't know as much about the business as you could. Increase your credibility and earn insiders' respect by becoming more knowledgeable.

Understand the competition for funds in a family business. More money for dividends and redemptions mean less for necessary reinvestment. Recognize the need for balance between your needs and what the business needs. Ultimately, insufficient reinvestment may stifle growth and mean less funds for dividends and redemptions. Think long term.

Make yourself financially independent of the business. Returns are nice, but if you are desperate for them, your desperation can skew the decisions of a sympathetic group of owners.

Find ways to get involved. You can become more connected to the family and the business if you take on a special role of some kind—such as volunteering for an owners' task force or a family committee. You needn't work in the business to feel a connection to it.

Don't meddle in the business. Leave the running of it up to those hired for the job.

Be trustworthy. Work to build trust between yourself and the insiders by behaving in trustful and trusting ways.

Owners, inside and outside the company, need to come together so that they can speak with one voice and move the business forward. The starting point is contained in that old, deceptively simple exhortation: walk a mile in each other's moccasins.

Other Insiders and Outsiders

Owners of stock in a family business should be sensitive to family members who do not own stock. This includes understanding the feelings of and being considerate of a spouse who does not own shares, as well as in-laws and blood relatives.

When one spouse owns shares and the other does not, feelings of inequality can result. The spouse who owns stock may feel that he or she has status they don't want. Non-owning spouses may feel like second-class citizens, or that they can't relate to a part of their spouses' lives. They might not be invited to shareholder meetings. If they are, they can't really speak up. If they do, they have to be extremely careful about what they say. In a sense, they have to subordinate themselves to the spouse's situation. An artificial distance is created between two people who would like to think that they share equal circumstances and equal life experience.

In the case of siblings or other blood relatives, some who are owners, as we have mentioned, will have feelings of unworthiness. Some who

The Owners' Pledge

- We pledge to treat one another with the utmost respect.
- We will be open and honest in our interactions with one another.
- We will put the welfare of the company and of the family ahead of our own.
- We will speak with one voice.
- We will educate ourselves to perform our duties to the best of our ability.
- We will strive to be independent of the family business for our financial support so as not to harm the business out of personal need.
- We will work to earn the trust of all other owners and extend our trust to them.
- We will communicate openly with one another.
- We will respect the role of management and the role of the board.
- We will adequately prepare the next generation for responsible and effective ownership.

---

are not owners will have feelings of resentment, wondering, "Why not me?" (Consider how, in many families, daughters have been barred from ownership simply because of gender.)

How non-owners are treated often depends on a family's culture. In some families, in-laws are treated like well-regarded trust beneficiaries. They don't have the power or the rights of a shareholder, but they are accepted as interested and influential parties. In other families, if you're not an owner, you're not an owner. Ownership business is kept strictly among owners, and your opinion and involvement are neither sought nor encouraged. Either approach can work.

If a family's culture permits, however, **we encourage keeping non-owners involved and informed, and finding opportunities for them to participate. Doing so is good for the family and, after all, the name of the non-owners is often on the door, too. They also want to be proud of the business that bears the family name. And they are parents of the next generation of owners.**

The same goes for trust beneficiaries and owners of non-voting stock, only more so. Such individuals have an economic interest in the business but no voting power. They feel distrusted and, in some cases, they ARE distrusted. To protect the business, one or more owners made sure that other family members would not have voting power when shares fell into their hands or would not have outright ownership at all.

When a family separates voting power from economic value, everyone in the family should understand and appreciate the reasons for the separation. Good reasons include increasing the chances for passing on the family business to future generations and estate planning considerations that make the separation desirable. The wise business family will put a lot of effort into preparing and educating family members about these issues, and the wise owners with voting power will be extremely empathetic toward those without. As suggested earlier, trust beneficiaries and non-voting owners should be treated with the same respect and attention given to voting owners. While they can't vote, they should still be provided with all the information that voting owners receive. They should be invited to participate in meetings and to represent the family or the business in the community. They should have a chance to express their opinions and to be heard.

Majority Versus Minority Shareholders

Don't underestimate the rights, the power, and the potential wrath of minority shareholders—or of non-voting shareholders, either. It is naive to assume that a minority shareholder is impotent. Minority owners treated with disrespect can exercise their rights and powers and make things very nasty. They can release information about the business. They can hire a lawyer and sue the company—doing considerable harm even if they don't win in court. Everything becomes very public, and the family is embarrassed.

At a conference not long ago, the adult daughters in one family told how they and their two siblings, all owners but without voting power, outwitted their mother. The family owned a resort. The mother and father had worked long and hard to make it a success and when the father died, the mother was exhausted. Unknown to the children, the mother, who held all the voting shares, decided to sell the business and entered into negotiations with a buyer.

When she told the children what she had done, they were furious. They were owners, after all, and felt they had a right to be consulted and to have a voice in the decision. Furthermore, they learned that the prospective buyer was not one they would want to take over their cherished business and were sure that the offer was too low. The children hired their own lawyer, but their real trump card was what they told their mother: "If you go through with this, you won't have a family anymore."

The mother backed down. Eventually, the business was sold, but to a buyer the children could accept and at much better terms.

The children in this case used power the mother didn't anticipate— emotional power. In other cases, less-powerful voting shareholders or trustees can form alliances that give them clout.

Again, **the more-powerful shareholders are best advised to treat the less-powerful ones as they would wish to be treated themselves.** How you as an owner treat less-powerful owners says a lot about your value system. Your children will quickly get a message that tells them whether you think minority shareholders are dismissible or are to be accorded fairness and dignity.

Ultimately, what brings the insiders and outsiders or the haves and have-nots together is trust. How to build trust? In addition to some of the simple steps we've suggested—be trustworthy; extend trust—**it's important to create systems and then to trust the systems to work.** We're thinking about such things as establishing a board that includes good independent directors, forming an ownership group to address ownership issues, setting up a family council, having family meetings, and formalizing the participation of spouses in family groups so that they feel more informed and connected.

It will also help if owners draft a shareholders pledge to help them transcend the issues described above and other issues discussed in this book. We offer a sample pledge here, but you will enjoy and learn from the process of crafting your own.

EXHIBIT 13

When You View
Shareholders As. . .   *The Outcome Will Be...*

When You View Shareholders As...	The Outcome Will Be...
"Parasites"	Loss of trust
"Spoiled"	Owners who fulfill your prophecy
"Greedy"	Owners who experience psychic costs
"Lacking in Knowledge"	Disaffected owners
"Knowledgeable"	Owners who actually are assets.
"Caring"	Effective Owners
"Committed"	Owners who reap psychic income
"Selfless"	Supportive owners

IX. Summary

After reading this booklet, do you find that ownership is different from what you thought it was? If so, that's not surprising. Ownership is often thought of in a narrow way when in fact, it has many dimensions.

Ownership ought to be an interesting, challenging, profitable, and spiritually enriching experience. And it can be, when you adopt an "ownership attitude" that is marked by a sense of stewardship toward the business you own and a deep respect for other shareholders.

There's nothing mysterious about being an owner. Effective ownership can be learned. No matter what your age, if you feel that you don't bring enough to the table to fulfill your responsibilities as an owner, you can educate yourself and gain the knowledge and skills to become a better owner.

The lessons of effective ownership can also be instilled in the members of the next generation from the time they are very young. Indeed, passing on the knowledge of what it means to be a good owner is one of the most important responsibilities of an effective owner. Family businesses that continue to succeed over time do so in large part because new generations of effective owners come along—not by accident but because they have been carefully prepared by previous generations of effective owners.

Effective ownership helps assure high-performing, long-lasting family businesses. And while being an effective owner won't assure that you as a human being live longer, your commitment to being effective and your efforts to fulfill that commitment will make you a higher-performing human being on many levels. You will find yourself thinking more consciously about values and finding ways to integrate them into this institution called a family business. You will be educating yourself and learning much that is fun to know and helpful to the business and the family. You will be monitoring your own behavior, asking yourself if this action or that decision serves the best interests of the family and of the business.

If, like so many owners, your ownership came to you as an inheritance, think of it as the gift that keeps on giving—giving you opportunities to grow, to do good in the family as well is in the business and the community, to enjoy a sense of purpose, and to gain a financial reward.

Glossary

Here are some terms that will be useful to new or inexperienced family business owners. Complete business dictionaries are suggested in the Suggested Readings and Resources section.

Balance Sheet. A statement representing the financial position of a company at a given point in time. It shows the company's assets (what the company owns and money owed to the company balanced against its liabilities (the money and obligations owed by a company, including the shareholders' equity).

Beneficiary. An individual named to receive the benefits of a trust.

Book Value. The worth of a company if all its assets were sold and its obligations paid off. Called "book" because it represents the value of assets or liabilities shown on a balance sheet or the company books. This is not to be confused with market value (see below).

Cash Flow. The movement of cash as it comes into a company in the form of sales and goes out in the form of purchases or overhead costs. A company can be in trouble when it has a negative cash flow (more money going out than coming in).

Fiduciary Duty. The responsibility legally imposed on an individual, a company, or an association entrusted to hold or invest money or other assets for a third party. A trustee has fiduciary responsibility to manage a trust in the best interest of the beneficiary. A board of directors has a fiduciary responsibility to the owners of a company.

Income Statement. A report that shows a company's revenues, expenses, and net income (profits) over a period of time—such as a year or a quarter. Often called a "profit and loss statement" (P&L) or a "statement of earnings."

Initial Public Offering (IPO). A company's first sale of shares to the public. Companies are said to "go public" when they offer some of their shares for sale through a stock exchange and cease to be completely privately owned.

Liquidity. The ability to turn assets into cash.

Market Value. The price at which a company or an asset can be sold. Often called "fair market value." It can be higher or lower than book value.

Net Worth. The value of a company's or an individual's assets minus liabilities—the same as "book value".

Profit and Loss Statement (P&L). See Income Statement.

Stakeholder. Any individual or entity that has an interest in the success of a company. Stakeholders can include shareholders, employees, suppliers, lenders, customers, and members of the community in which a business is located.

Trust. A legal entity that holds assets for the benefit of an individual or an organization. A trustee is named by the trustor (creator) to manage the trust for a specific purpose. In family businesses, shares may be put into a trust for the benefit of certain family members (the beneficiaries) or to vote the shares as a group—a voting trust.

Trustee. An individual or institution appointed to oversee a trust according to the instructions of the trust's creator. A trustee has a fiduciary duty to manage a trust in the best interest of the beneficiary.

Voting Trust. A trust in which some shareholders give their voting rights to one or more other shareholders, called "voting trustees."

Suggested Readings and Resources

Books:
Act Like an Owner: Building an Ownership Culture, by Robert M. Blonchek and Martin F. O'Neill (John Wiley & Sons, Inc., 1999). Describes what an "ownership culture" is in a company and how business leaders can achieve it.

Arthur Andersen Answers the 101 Toughest Questions About Family Business, by Barbara B. Buchholz, Margaret Crane, and Ross W. Nager (Prentice Hall Press, 2000). Provides an overview of family business in a useful question-and-answer format.

How To Read a Financial Report, by John A. Tracy (Fifth Edition, John Wiley & Sons, Inc., 1999). Takes the mystery out of balance sheets, income statements, cash flow, statements, and other financial measures and terms.

Strategic Planning for the Family Business: Parallel Planning to Unify the Family and Business, by Randel S. Carlock and John L. Ward (Palgrave, 2001). Shows family business owners how they can work with management to make the best strategic choices for the business and the family.

Word Smart for Business, by Paul Westbrook (Random House, Inc., 1999). Defines more than 4,000 business terms in easy-to-understand language. Also useful is the *Dictionary of Business Terms,* edited by Jack P. Friedman, (Third Edition published in 2000 by Barron's Educational Series, Inc.).

Periodicals:

The Family Business Advisor, a monthly newsletter published by Family Enterprise Publishers and Andersen Center for Family Business, P.O. Box 4356, Marietta, GA 30061-4356 (1-800-551-0633). A monthly newsletter containing useful information about family business and family business ownership.

The Wall Street Journal, the national business newspaper published five times a week by Dow Jones, Inc. (www.wsj.com). An excellent source of general business information and trends.

Web Sites:

www.ceoexpress.com. A portal to business information and media of all kinds—from *Forbes* and *Fortune* to local business journals.

www.entreworld.org. An educational site sponsored by the Kauffman Center for Entrepreneurial Leadership. Key word searches on "family business," "ownership," or the business concept of your choice can lead to scores of useful articles.

Index

The Authors

Craig E. Aronoff, Ph.D.

Co-founder and principal of The Family Business Consulting Group, Inc., Craig Aronoff is a leading consultant, speaker, writer, and educator in the family business field.

As the founder of the Cox Family Enterprise Center at Kennesaw State University in Marietta, GA, Aronoff invented and implemented the membership-based, professional-service-provider sponsored Family Business Forum, which has served as a model of family business education for some 150 universities world-wide. Until his retirement in January 2005, he held the Dinos Eminent Scholar Distinguished Chair of Private Enterprise and was a professor of management in Kennesaw State's Coles College of Business.

As a consultant, Aronoff has worked with hundreds of family companies in the U.S. and abroad on issues including generational transitions; developing business and family governance processes and structures; finding and articulating family missions and values; facilitating decision making and conflict resolution; managerial development; family compensation and dividend policies; family meetings; and more. As an inspiring, informative and entertaining speaker on a variety of family business topics, he speaks regularly to trade and professional groups and has lectured at over 100 universities.

Aronoff is perhaps the most prolific writer in the family business field. He has authored, co-authored or been editor of more than thirty books, including the 20-volume *Family Business Leadership Series* and is executive editor of *The Family Business Advisor*.

Listed in *Who's Who* and widely acknowledged for his work in the area of family business, Aronoff has received, among other honors: the Family Firm Institute's Beckhard Award for Outstanding Contributions to Family Business Practice; The Freedom Foundation's Leavey Award for Excellence in Private Enterprise Education; and the National Federation of Independent Business Foundation's Outstanding Educator Award. The Aronoff Professorship of Family Business at Kennesaw State University was named in his honor.

Aronoff grew up in a family business. He received his bachelor's degree from Northwestern University, his Masters from the University of Pennsylvania, and his Doctorate from the University of Texas at Austin.

John L. Ward, Ph.D.

John L. Ward, Ph.D. is a co-founder of The Family Business Consulting Group, Inc.7, clinical professor at Kellogg School of Management and Wild Group Professor of Family Business at IMD. Ward teaches strategic management, business leadership and family enterprise continuity. He is an active researcher, speaker and consultant on family succession, ownership, governance and philanthropy.

He is the author of many leading texts on family business including, *Keeping the Family Business Healthy*, *Creating Effective Boards for Private Enterprises*, *Strategic Planning for the Family Business* and *Perpetuating the Family Business: 50 Lessons Learned from Long-Lasting Successful Families in Business*. He is also co-author of a collection of booklets, *The Family Business Leadership Series*, each focusing on specific issues family businesses face.

Ward graduated from Northwestern University (B.A.) and Stanford Graduate School of Business (M.B.A. and Ph.D.). He is the co-director of The Center for Family Enterprises at Kellogg and currently serves on the boards of several companies in the U.S. and Europe. He conducts regular seminars in Spain, Italy, India, Hong Kong, Sweden, and Switzerland.

John and his wife, Gail, a Chicago high school principal, live in Evanston, Illinois. They have two adult children. They are active in community and educational activities and enjoy family travel and sports.